An English Heritage Handbook

Upnor Castle

KENT

A D SAUNDERS MA, FSA, FRHistS
Chief Inspector of Ancient Monuments and Historic Buildings

First published 1967
Previously published by HMSO 1983
First published by English Heritage (The Historic Buildings and
Monuments Commission for England) 1985
Reprinted 1987

Published by English Heritage and printed in England for HMSO by Taylor Bloxham Ltd
Dd 8975231 C5 6/87
ISBN 1 85074 039 9

Contents

Like virtue it is, to save that is got
As to get the thing, that earst she had not
Who gave me this shew, to none other ende
But strongly to stand, her Navie to defend

Lambarde, *Perambulation of Kent,* third edition

History

View from Upnor towards Sheerness, by J Farington RA, 1795

Introduction

More than any other Tudor castle, Upnor has close ties with the navy. It was built expressly for the protection of Queen Elizabeth's warships anchoring in the Medway, and its importance matched the growth of the dockyards at Chatham. Even after it had served out its military usefulness the castle retained its naval connection as a magazine supplying gunpowder and munitions to the men-of-war riding in the river or off the Nore.

The Medway has the advantage of slow-running water with a good rise and fall of the tide. The channel is free of rocks and lies between low-lying banks, with shelter from southwest winds provided by the surrounding hills. As there are no strong currents, ships could be grounded for repairs. Defensively, the existence of 10 miles (16km) of sinuous sand and mudbanks between the mouth of the estuary and Gillingham Reach made the unpiloted navigation of a sailing ship in any but a fair wind a dangerous enterprise.

No doubt for these reasons the upper reaches of the Medway, below Rochester Bridge, became increasingly valuable for laying-up Henry VIII's navy when 'in ordinary,' or out of commission. Gradually the anchorage became more used and in 1547 payment was made for the hire of a storehouse in Gillingham. From these insignificant origins sprang the future of Chatham Yard. More storehouses were built, and land was hired for making a mast dock. Although there was no dry-dock at Chatham until the reign of James I, before long Chatham had joined the ranks with Woolwich and Deptford with their shipbuilding and repair yards on the Thames. The Medway served as a nursery for seamen. The young Francis Drake grew up here with his father, a sailor and an advanced Protestant, who, driven from the West Country, found a place as a lay preacher in a hulk at Chatham.

By 1564 twenty-three of the largest ships of the Queen's fleet, nearly the whole of it in fact, were moored below Rochester Bridge. Some form of protection was obviously needed as the ships, without sails and rigging, were sitting birds at the mercy of a bold enemy raid up river. There had been no tradition of coastal defence here in medieval times: the massive castle at Rochester guarded the bridge crossing, while the fourteenth-century castle at Queenborough protected Sheppey rather than the Medway estuary. In Henry VIII's castle-building programme, when the Thames was provided with five BLOCKHOUSES, only one was built at Sheerness, but in those days the importance of the river to the navy had not been appreciated. [See the Glossary for an explanation of the terms printed in SMALL CAPITALS.]

Building the castle (1559–67)

It was in 1559, the year after Elizabeth's accession, that the Queen and the Privy Council ordered a BULWARK to be built at Upnor. Six 'indifferent persons' examined the banks of the river and chose the site. It belonged to Mr Thomas Devinisshe of Frindsbury, and in the same year the office of the Treasurer of Marine Causes was instructed to pay the owner £25 for six acres of land or thereabouts.

The designer was Sir Richard Lee, for long the foremost English military engineer of his day. Apart from drawing the plan and recommending the composition of the labour force and the general lines the work should take, he has only a shadowy part in the building history. Undoubtedly he was much too occupied with the construction of the monumental defences of Berwick-on-Tweed to pay Upnor much attention. His deputy was Humphrey Locke, who was described as the overseer, surveyor and chief carpenter.

The man responsible for the day-to-day management and accountancy was Richard Watts. He is one of the best remembered of Rochester's citizens. Prominent in the city's affairs, a former mayor and founder of almshouses, he has his memorial both in the cathedral and in the buildings with which he was connected in life. To be chosen as paymaster, clerk of the store and purveyor at Upnor Castle must have been due to his years as government contractor and victualler to the navy. He has sometimes been claimed as the architect but since he was only being paid two shillings a day to Humphrey Locke's two shillings and sixpence this cannot be so.

There seem to have been at least two designs before Lee's castle took shape. The building was certainly not so extensive as the present structure. Initially it consisted of the great, angled, water BASTION and the rectangular residential block built over and against the river bank. There was also some form of tower at either end of the walled water frontage. The gatehouse and moat were added later and the courtyard wall and the two towers at either end of the water front were drastically rebuilt. There was, in this first castle, ample space to mount the great guns, both on the bastion and on top of the main building.

Richard Watts' account lasts from 1559 to 1564. Its largest single items were the sums paid for stone and the wages of the masons and handhewers (quarrymen). About a third as much was spent on bricks but few bricklayers were employed. The next largest payments were to the lime burners and choppers of chalk, closely followed by the carpenters. Timber, ironwork and tools accounted for other large sums. Included were 90 tons of oak, much of it taken from the woods of Sir Thomas Wyatt near Aylesford. Some of the timber was the surplus following the building of another blockhouse at Sheerness. The accounts illustrate the variety of equipment and material needed on a building site, even such everyday items as wheelbarrows, shovels and spades. The quantities of stone included rubble and ASHLAR, some of the dressed stone being worked in the quarry. As might be expected in Kent, many loads of ragstone were bought by the ton and by the yard. Some of the stone came from Rochester Castle, for the labourers were not only employed at Upnor, but also at Rochester Castle, Aylesford and Bopley, pulling down buildings for material, transporting it to and from the waterside as well as loading and unloading the ships and the land transport. So much material was brought by water that storehouses and wharfage had to be hired at Rochester. In all, £3621 was spent.

Early in 1561 the Queen was impatiently writing to the Lord Admiral demanding that the bulwark at Upnor should be completed. It is clear that the main structure had been erected by 1564 but progress lagged until three years later when a further £728 was spent in finishing it. The materials bought illustrate how far the earlier building campaign had progressed. Stone for chimneys, windows and two LOOPS was required. Timber boards are more frequent and 'small coales to make black mortar for the chimneys,' bricks and paving tile, laths, lime and hair for the internal finishing, 169ft (51.5m) of glass and, most significant of all, £253 was spent on lead, more than the cost of all the other items put together. This clearly means the roofing of the main building. As a final touch the painters gilded the lion which acted as a weather vane on top of the stairs. Richard Watts was now completely in control. Perhaps Humphrey Locke had died in the interval, for he is only recorded as having made two journeys to these later works.

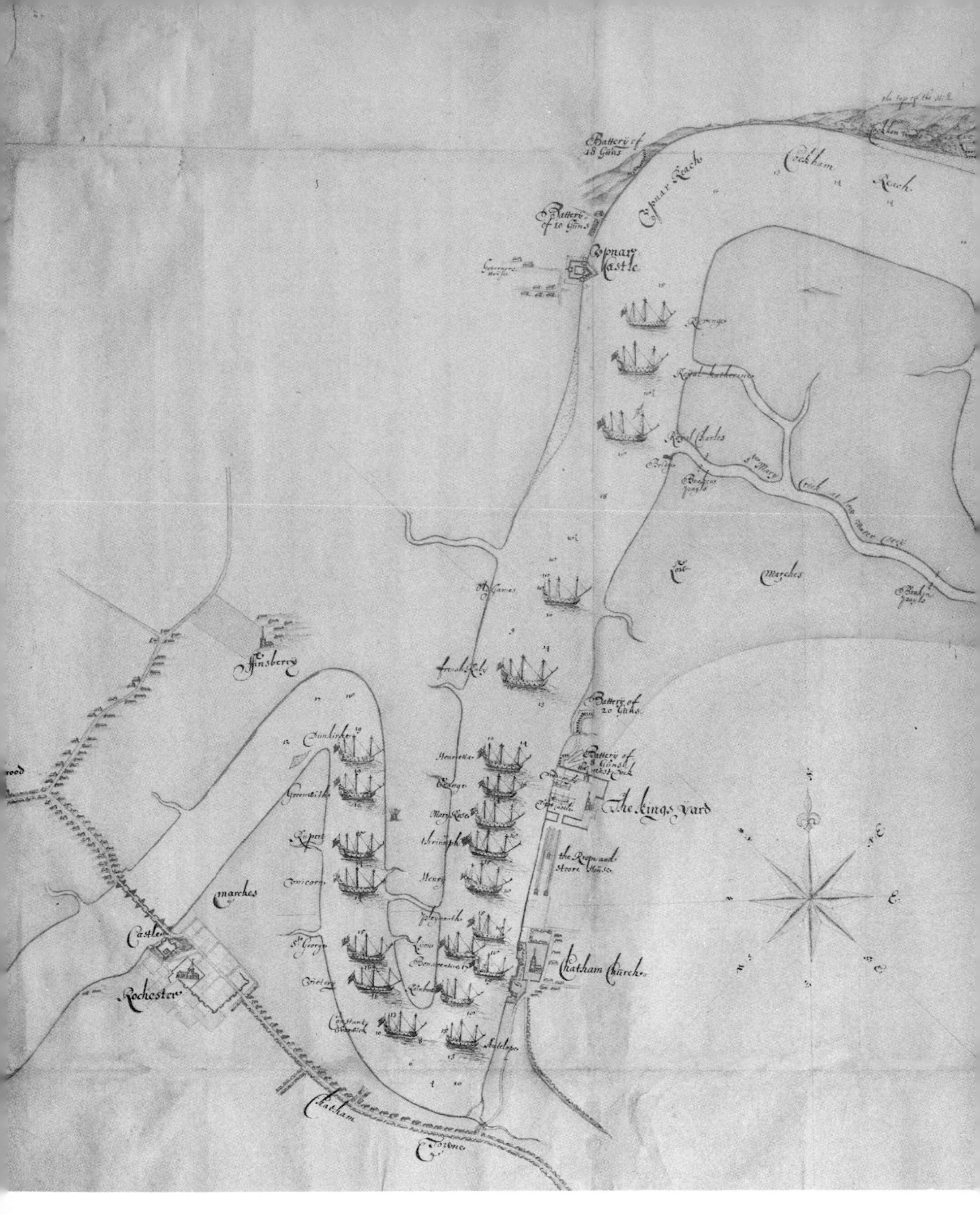

The River of Chatham with the new Batteryes made by Sir Bernard de Gomme, 1669

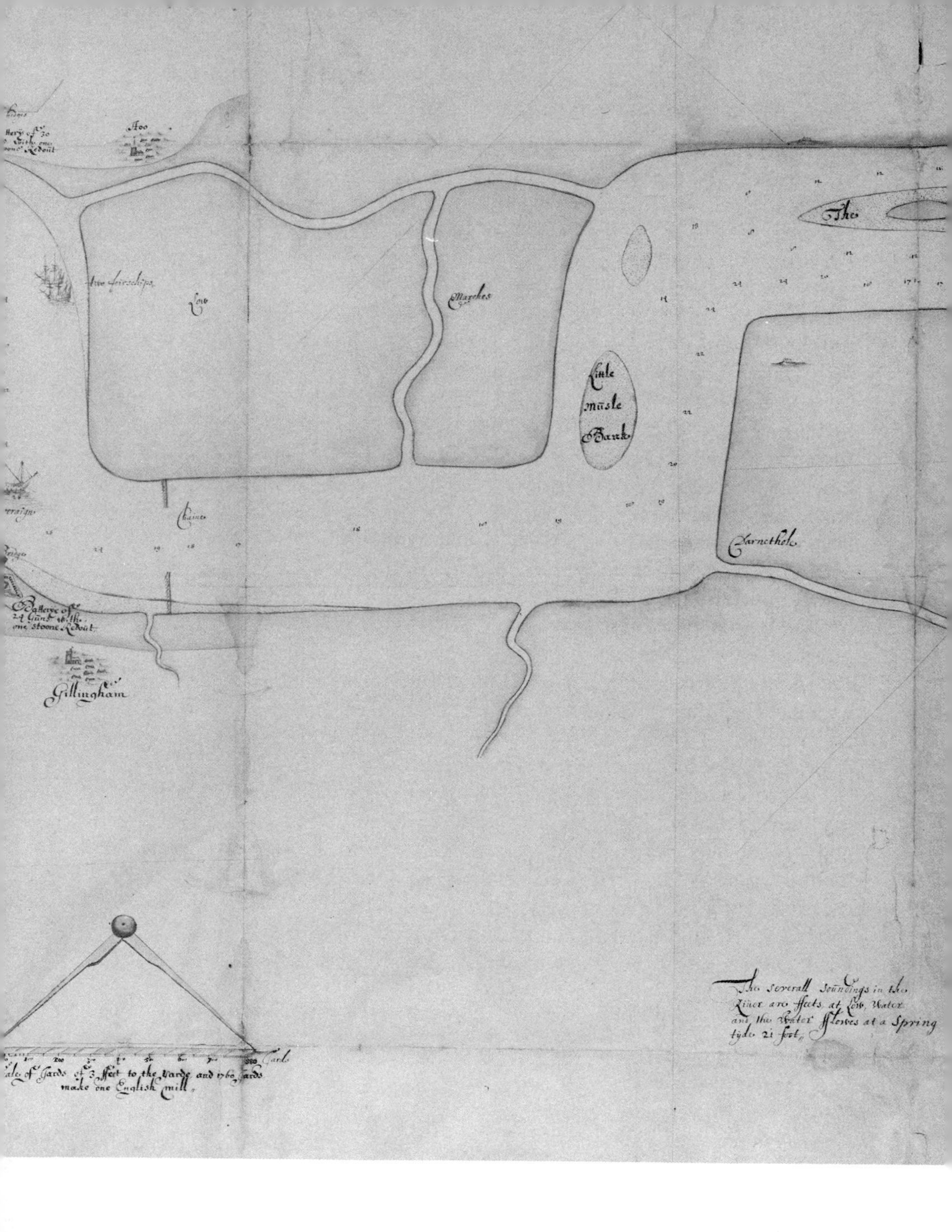

two fireschips
Low
Marches
Little
mūsle
Bank
Chaine
Battery of
24 Guns with
one stoone Redout
Gillingham
The
The severall Soundings in the
River are ffeets at Low Water
and the Water fflowes at a Spring
tyde 21 foot
of Yards of 3 ffeet to the Yarde and 1760 yards
make one English mill

Elizabethan defensive measures in the Medway

The more the Medway was used the greater grew the fears for the shipping at anchor there and the valuable naval stores at Chatham. Relations with Spain were always strained, and for about twenty years there was a period which we should call today 'cold war' before hostilities broke out in earnest. The Medway was open to a raid from the Spanish-controlled ports of the Low Countries, and rumours and alarms were frequent.

Eventually Sir William Winter, Surveyor of the Navy, examined the defensive problems and surprisingly rejected Sheerness and the Isle of Grain for additional fortification in favour of a fort at Swaleness, opposite Queenborough. This was to prevent a raid from the rear by way of the Swale. He also thought it would be better to move the ships from Chatham to Queenborough if docks could be made for them. Swaleness Fort was erected in 1575, and the precaution was taken of blocking with piles the passage through St Mary's Creek by which the Upnor anchorage could be taken in the flank. Ships were stationed off Sheerness to protect the estuary and examine all passing shipping.

In 1585, when open war with Spain had begun, a chain was stretched across the river below the castle with timber work on both sides of the river. A few years before, William Bourne, while master gunner at Upnor (1579–80), had prepared a memorandum on means of protecting the navy. His view was that it was fallacious to trust heavy guns to repel invading ships. Their sails and rigging would be damaged but they would not be sunk. He went on to explain the advantages of a chain. A drawing of about this date shows the ships moored athwart the stream in three groups between Rochester Bridge and Upnor Castle, the largest vessel being near Upnor. Three years later, in Armada year, maintenance of the chain cost £80 and the garrison in the castle included six gunners and a master gunner. Later, in 1596, it seems to have been inadequately manned. Lord Admiral Howard reported that the castle should either be well garrisoned or pulled down in order to deny it to an enemy who might land and surprise it. He suggested that fifty trained men should guard it and a month later its garrison comprised eighty men who each received 8d a day.

Enlargement of the castle (1599–1601)

At the end of the sixteenth century came the additions which were to give the castle its present shape. In October 1599 Sir John Leveson's estimate of £761-9s-10d for new work was accepted, and a plan was sent indicating the position of a timber PALISADE which was urgently needed in front of the bastion. The plan also showed an enclosing ditch with FLANKERS to cover it, and the bastion, or great platform, was to be raised 'with a parapet of good height to be furnished with loopes for great ORDNANCE.' It was declared that serviceable stone could be got at Rochester Castle. One hundred and sixty trees were requisitioned in the Hundred of Axstone. A furious complaint ensued because an enthusiastic official marked down 100 of these trees on land belonging to a Mr Lovelace. 'I almost well like of the indiscreet dealing therein,' wrote the Lord Admiral's office to Sir John Leveson while acknowledging that this was an unfair burden for one man to bear.

By May 1600 the palisade was finished, the ditch had been dug to a depth of 18ft (5.5m) and was 32ft (9.8m) wide, repairs had been made to the great platform over the main building, the gatehouse and DRAWBRIDGE with the engine to raise it had been erected and the stonework for the new parapet for the water bastion had been brought from Bocton quarry and was lying nearby. This had taken nearly all the estimated £761. Still needing to be done were the actual laying of the new parapet, building the flankers at each end of the ditch, which itself required turfing, and bringing water into the castle. An additional £380 was asked for and obtained. The engineer in charge of the work, Arthur Gregory, though efficient in pressing on with the work, was a disgruntled man. His letters to Sir John Leveson are full of complaints about deficiencies in pay and ill health. It seems that an Italian engineer, Baptist, may have advised on design.

The work went on until 3 September 1601, when Sir John Leveson presented his account. The flankers at each end of the ditch had been built and their dimensions tally with the ground floors of the present North and South Towers although the rounded turrets towards the river seem to have belonged to Lee's design. The ditch was turfed and the timber platforms on either side of the tower (probably on the main building) were replaced and covered with lead. In the accounts a motley collection of materials is mentioned down to the cord for setting out the ditch. Various contractors were brought in for particular jobs. John Banester dug and brought by water 612 tons of ragstone and 223 tons of ashlar from Rochester Castle. The same contractor made the vault below the north flanker and the vaulted passage between the North Tower and the main building as well as raising the earlier parapet. He also dug the well, 36ft (11m) deep. Nicholas White, a joiner, repaired the hall and the dining chamber of the castle. Thomas Andrews built a timber-framed stable with lodgings over it. The total spent in these two years was £1137-3s-5d. But the castle was still in an unfinished state. Another £68 was requested for finishing the necessary works. The castle in plan, though not in elevation, had achieved something of its appearance today.

Early seventeenth century

J Linewraye, in a survey of ORDNANCE, wrote of Upnor in 1603: 'The Castle of Upnor and two SCONCES there situate, for the guarding and defence of the same your most Royall Navy; wherein I dare averre that no Kinge in Europe is able to equall your excellent Majeste,' possessed a demi-cannon, 7 culverin, 5 demi-culverin, a minion, a falcon, a saker and 4 fowlers with 2 chambers apiece. Warham Sconce had 2 culverin and 5 demi-culverin; Bay Sconce had 4 demi-culverin.

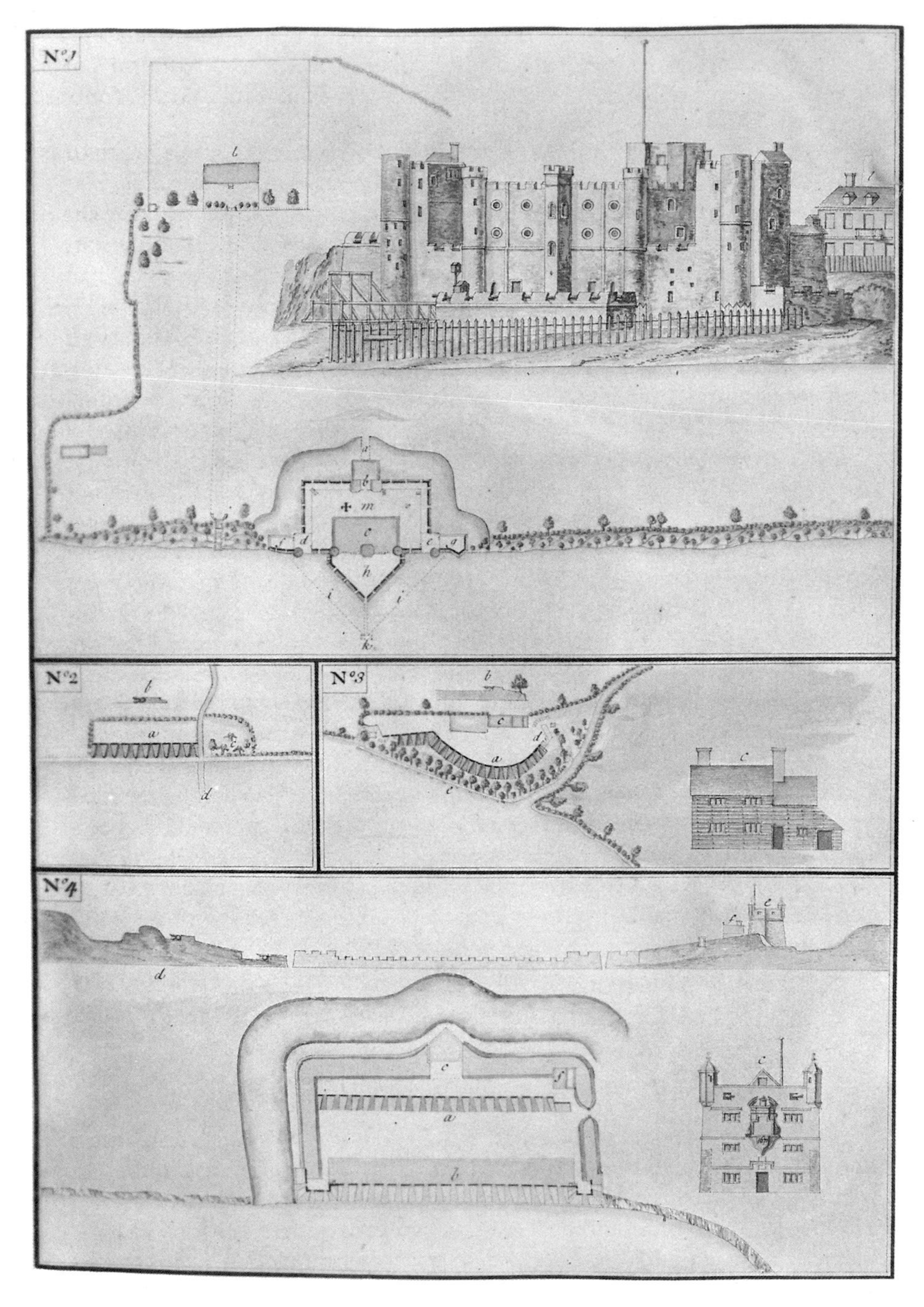

Plan and elevations, 1698

Twenty years later, another survey noted that at Upnor eighteen guns of various sizes were mounted. Among the unserviceable equipment at that time were thirty-four longbows, an indication that this traditional weapon retained its value well into the late sixteenth century. The garrison consisted of a captain, a master gunner paid sixteen pence a day, seven gunners at a shilling a day and twenty soldiers at eight pence. The BOOM DEFENCE of a chain worked by two great wheels continued in use but its position tended to move further and further downstream.

The survey of 1623 also listed the repairs that were necessary. The drawbridge and its mechanism were broken, various platforms needed renewing and it would seem that the old wall enclosing the courtyard had finally collapsed. A new CURTAIN WALL was necessary to protect the gunners on the battery from being picked off from the rear.

At the outbreak of the Civil War in 1642, Upnor Castle and the two sconces were surrendered to Parliament who garrisoned them. They had an uneventful war, serving as a prison for Royalist officers. But in the sudden rising in Kent, on behalf of the Royalists, in 1648, the castle was seized. The insurrection, however, was soon suppressed and the governor of the castle, Major Brown, returned to his post. Then, following a visit by the Parliamentary general, Fairfax, more repairs were put in hand. Inevitably the gun PLATFORMS wanted renewing and from this account it appears that two platforms existed on the main building as well as others on the two towers. At this time the gatehouse was without a platform. All this work was estimated to cost £101 but rather more was done since in 1650 a warrant for £673-2s-4d was issued to reimburse Major Brown for money spent on repairs.

The nature of this work is perhaps indicated by the happenings three years later. Early in 1653 the then Governor petitioned the Admiralty for the repair of the gatehouse which had caught fire, destroying five soldiers' rooms, and 'for covering the North Tower built by Major Brown and left uncovered.' The presence of bricklayers to the exclusion of masons in the accounts and the large sum spent by Major Brown suggest that the heightening of the gatehouse in brick must be attributable to this period. The open back of the North Tower was also built up in brick in order to make it suitable for accommodation. The similar enclosing of the South Tower probably came soon after.

Dutch raid of 1667

It was not until Upnor's last days as a fortress that it was called upon for action in defence of the fleet. This was during the Second Dutch War. In 1667, after a victorious sea battle, the English Government felt that there was little more to fear from the Dutch for a time and decided to economise by keeping the fleet at home and relying on fortifications for defence. But against all expectations the Dutch put to sea again and in June, under the command of de Ruyter, a squadron appeared in the Thames, reaching Gravesend. De Ruyter then decided to strike at Chatham and, as a preliminary, attacked and burnt the unfinished new fort at Sheerness.

The Duke of Albemarle, arriving to take charge of the defences, found Chatham in panic. The chain was in position, now between Hoo Ness and Gillingham, and he threw up two BATTERIES—one at each end of the chain—and made an ineffective attempt to block the channel. On the morning of 12 June the leading Dutch ships bore down on the chain. Whether it broke or was cast loose by a Dutch landing party is uncertain, but it proved no obstacle. The *Royal Charles* was carried off and other ships were burnt. There is little doubt that had the attack been pushed home with more vigour the dockyard and every ship might have been destroyed. The Dutch anchored when the tide turned and did not resume operations until the next day; in the interval Albemarle planted guns in suitable positions and constructed an eight-gun battery (Middleton's Battery) beside Upnor Castle. When the Dutch came forward again they were brought under heavy artillery and musketry fire from Upnor. More shipping, however, was burnt but the Dutch could not progress and eventually retired to Queenborough where they remained for some days before putting to sea.

On 24 July a belated royal warrant ordered that Upnor was henceforth to be kept as 'a fort and place of strength.' The Peace of Breda seven days later set the seal on what was a most ignominious defeat. The diarist, Evelyn, visiting Chatham soon afterwards and looking at the burnt-out hulks, described it as 'a Dreadful Spectacle as ever any English men saw and a dishonour never to be wiped off.'

Upnor Castle had acquitted itself well, at least in the popular mind. Pepys (the diarist and Secretary to the Admiralty) said 'I do not see that Upnor Castle hath received any hurt by them though they played long against it; and they themselves shot till they had hardly a gun left upon the carriages, so badly provided they were.' Lack of munitions, not courage, was Upnor's failing.

Fortification of the Medway

The humiliation of the Medway raid led to a revision of England's coastal defences, particularly for the protection of naval ports. For the next fifteen years enormous sums of money were spent at Plymouth, Portsmouth, Hull, Tynemouth and in the Thames and Medway. Many of these fortifications were designed by the chief engineer and leading expert of the day, Sir Bernard de Gomme.

A bastioned fort was built at Sheerness to protect the guns at Garrison Point and the beginnings of the dockyard there. Part of these seventeenth-century defences survives today among the fortification of later centuries. But, as well as defending the entrance to the Medway, more protection for the anchored shipping in Chatham and Long Reach was needed. De Gomme therefore designed two forts on either side of the river: at Cockham Wood, about 1 mile (1.6km) below Upnor Castle, and at Gillingham, at the entrance to the former St Mary's Creek. He came down in 1669 with Jonas Moore, another engineer, and spent four days staking them out. They were really powerful gun batteries, with square three-storey towers inside them. The site of Gillingham Fort has been built over but traces of Cockham Wood Fort still survive.

Late seventeenth-century plans show the need for further protection as the largest ships of the fleet had to be moored well below Upnor, and the long line of vessels now reached past Hoo Ness. More batteries were built, at Hoo Ness itself and as far down river as the Isle of Grain. The old boom defence continued for some years but when a new chain was proposed in 1688, and the Admiralty was still hankering for one ten years later, the Navy Board was unsympathetic and claimed the new batteries were a more efficient protection.

Fortress into Magazine

These defensive revisions reduced Upnor's importance. The renowned bulwark against the Dutch was in fact already redundant. In 1668 it was ordered to be converted into 'a Place of Stores and Magazine.' To some extent this was a recognition of a change of function which had already developed. The year before, hundreds of barrels of gunpowder were being shipped by HOY from the Tower of London wharf to Upnor. Later, there are many mentions of barrels of CORNPOWDER, generally more than 300 at a time, being taken out to various warships anchored off the buoy at the Nore or sometimes in the Swale off Queenborough. Thus began Upnor's long history as a magazine for supplying munitions to the navy.

Changes to the building must have been made about this time, involving a general heightening of the main building and the North and South Towers and the removal of the gun platforms on the roof. But the new work retained the castellated appearance. The storekeeper's house was built and still stands as part of Castle House. By 1698 Upnor Castle looked very much as it does now.

A survey in 1691 of the ordnance, carriages and munitions at the various forts in the country shows how important Upnor had become in this new role. There were 164 iron guns, 62 standing carriages. 100 ships' carriages, 7125 round shot, 4 MATCHLOCK MUSKETS, and 200 SNAPHAUNCE MUSKETS, 77 pikes and 5206 barrels of cornpowder. No other establishment had so much powder in store. The Tower of London had the next largest stock with 3692 barrels. Four years later, a statement of repairs shows something of the way the conversion had affected the castle. There was a flat lead roof over the powder rooms in the main building and 9in (228mm) square posts were needed to support the beams of the first floor which had begun to sag with the weight of the powder.

Until 1827 the castle continued to be a magazine. New building was carried out and alterations and repairs were made. To the southwest the barracks was built soon after 1718; a century later it could provide accommodation for two officers and sixty-four soldiers. Gradually other storehouses grew up on land to the north. In 1778 Hasted wrote '. . .it is many years past since a gun was mounted there.' For the security of the Powder Magazine there was a Governor, Storekeeper, Clerk of the Cheque, Master Gunner and twelve other Gunners. There was also an Officer Commanding soldiers on detachment, which with the rest of the forts on the river except Sheerness, were under the command of the Governor of Upnor. These forts, Bird's Nest, Cockham Wood, Hoo Ness Fort had no guns mounted and were ruinous. The South Tower of Upnor Castle is allowed to the Governor for his house for he never lives there because of its poor condition.' Prints of that time show the water bastion roofed and part of the magazine establishment, with only a memory of its former armed strength.

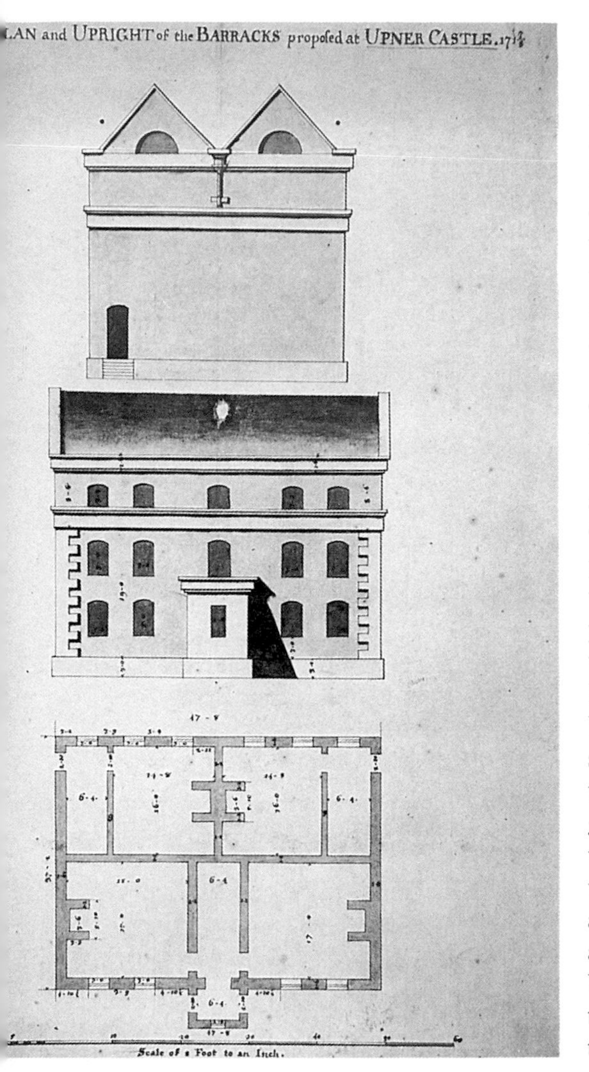

Plan and elevation of the Barracks, 1717-18. From Kings Topographical Collection XVIII

Garrison life went on, full of minor events and undisturbed by any major issues. When a ship arrived at the Blackstakes in the Lower Medway some of the respective officers at Chatham would go aboard to take the powder out. It then went to Upnor where it was sifted and COOPERED and put into the magazine. Its condition was then reported to the Ordnance Board. The master gunner visited each barrack each day at 10 pm in the summer and 9 pm in the winter to see that all lights were out and every gunner in bed. In 1746 the soldiers were described as 'a sett of drunken wretches.' Indeed the storekeeper asked for some railings to be set up about 12ft (3.7m) in front of the barracks to prevent them falling over the cliff. In acute cases of drunkenness the offender was imprisoned in the

'Black Hole.' In 1689 it was rumoured that the governor harboured papists and that an ensign at the castle had drunk damnation to the Prince of Orange in the White Hart at Rochester, but these seem to be extraordinary scandals in an otherwise humdrum existence.

Two of the castle's occupants did acquire a certain fame in the field of navigational theory. William Bourne, a prolific writer on navigation and gunnery, was master gunner at the castle in 1579–80, and Robert Heath wrote *Astronomica Accurata* there in 1760.

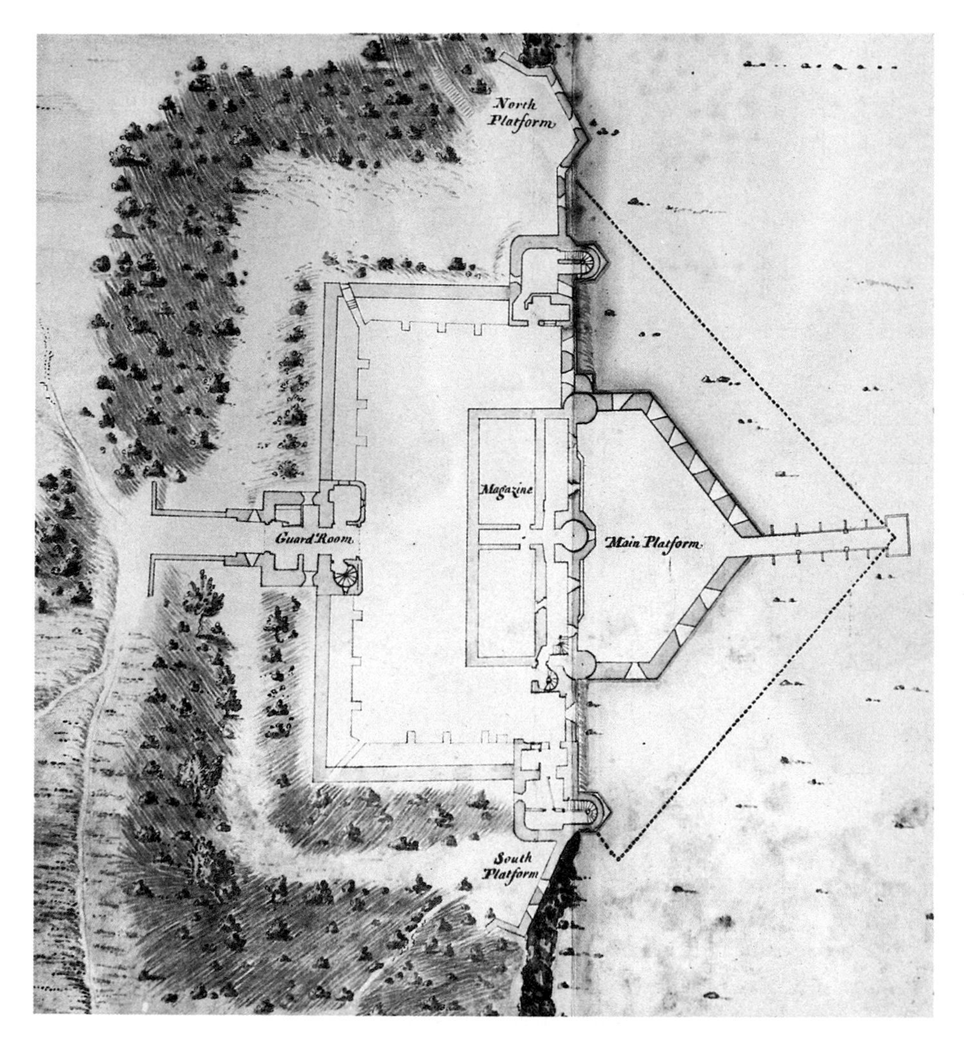

Plan of 1725. From Kings Topographical Collection XVIII

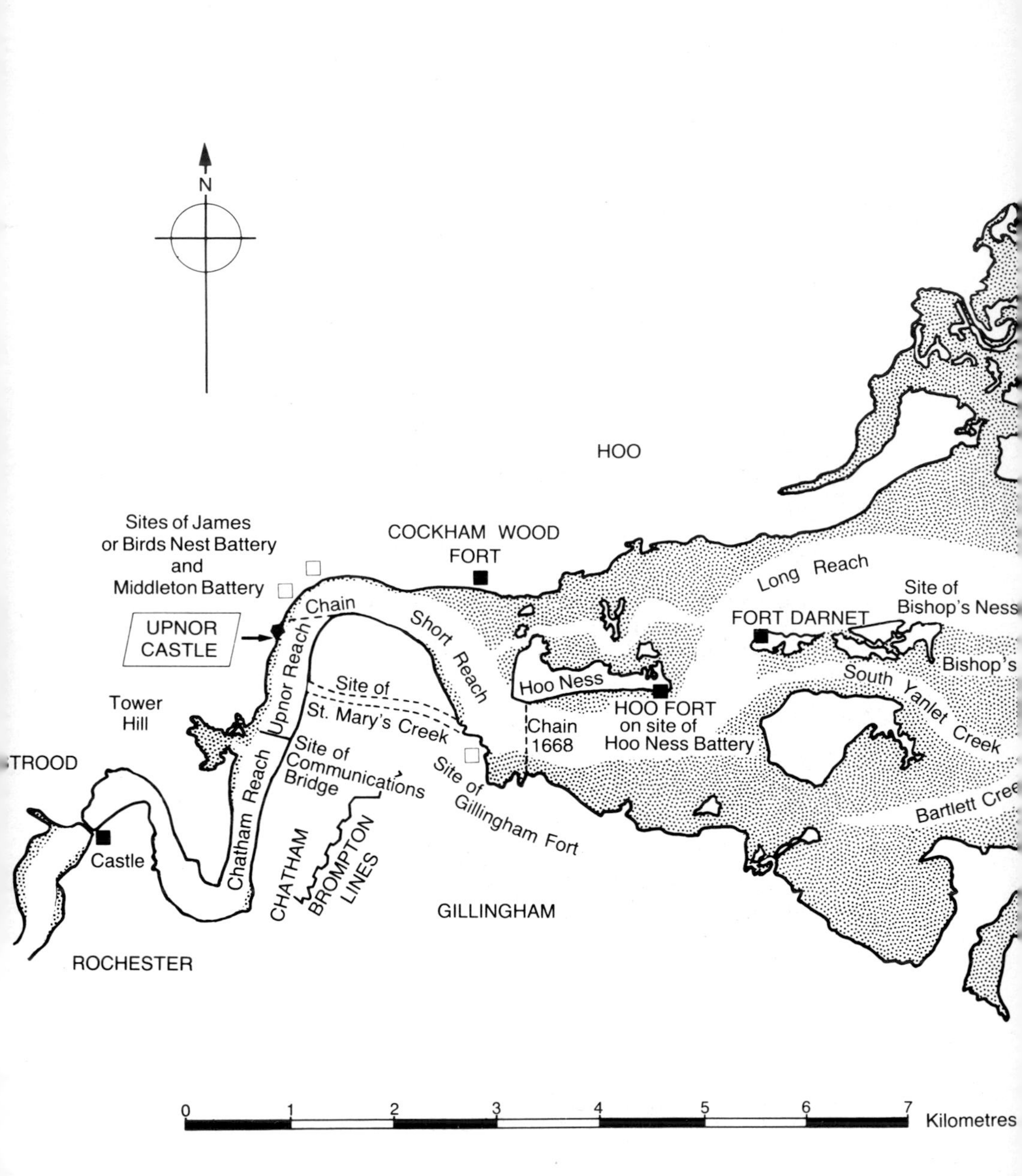

The Medway and its fortifications

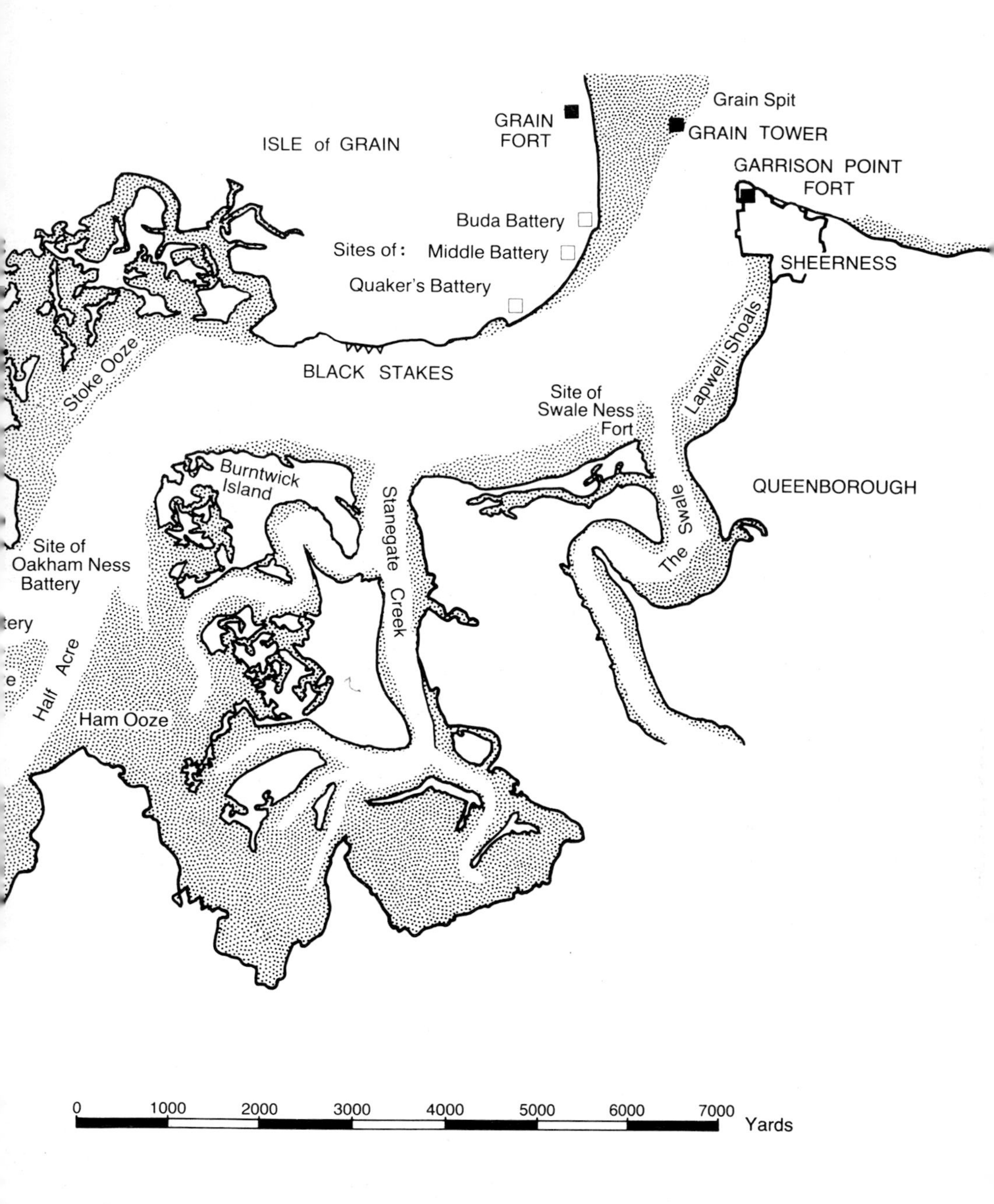
Grain Spit
GRAIN FORT
GRAIN TOWER
ISLE of GRAIN
GARRISON POINT FORT
Buda Battery
Sites of:
Middle Battery
Quaker's Battery
SHEERNESS
Stoke Ooze
BLACK STAKES
Lapwell Shoals
Site of Swale Ness Fort
Burntwick Island
Stanegate Creek
QUEENBOROUGH
The Swale
Site of Oakham Ness Battery
Half Acre
Ham Ooze
0
1000
2000
3000
4000
5000
6000
7000
Yards

Drawing from the river, 1780. From Kings Topographical Collection XVIII

Watercolour sketch from MS of Thomas Pennant's 'Outlines of the Globe,' volume XX, 1787

Later history

After 1827 Upnor ceased to be a magazine and was fitted up as an Ordnance Laboratory. By 1840 it contained no stocks of gunpowder or explosives. Magazines continued to be built outside to the north. Later Chattenden Barracks was built originally as the School of Military Railways and a railway was laid in 1872–73 between it and Upnor. This was relaid in 1885 at 2ft 6in (76cm) gauge for steam locomotives. More magazines were built at Lodge Hill just after the turn of the century.

The dockyard at Chatham was also expanding. It eventually spread across St Mary's Creek, blocking the view down the Medway from the castle. The prison hulks which had been anchored in the river for much of the early nineteenth century off Upnor and which had been part of the scene were gradually towed away.

The defence of the Medway continued to be a matter of great concern. In 1860 the Royal Commission on the Defence of the United Kingdom planned a thorough revision and the building of new fortifications began soon afterwards. At the estuary mouth, the two-tiered CASEMATED fortress at Garrison Point loomed massively on the Sheerness side, matched by batteries on the Isle of Grain. A long earthwork and wet moat, the Queenborough Lines, protected Sheerness from attack from the rear. In the Medway itself the earlier batteries covering the channel were replaced by the twin forts of Hoo and Darnet, which to an incoming warship must have seemed like Scylla and Charybdis. Built on mud flats, each had eleven heavy guns in casemates. The barracks and dockyard at Chatham had been fortified in the eighteenth century by the Brompton Lines. By the end of the nineteenth century, the Medway towns were ringed on the south and east by detached forts.

In 1891 Upnor and its depot were transferred from the War Office to the Admiralty. Prior to this, although the Admiralty made financial provision, the War Office had made arrangements for the storage, upkeep and supply of the Armament Stores for the Navy. Now the Naval Armament Supply Department was formed. The castle was used for various purposes and the bastion and courtyard were PROOFYARDS. Gradually the castle came to be treated more and more as a museum. It was finally recognised as such in 1945 after having served as part of the Magazine Establishment during the war. It was damaged by two bombs which fell in the garden of Upnor House in 1941. Thereafter a certain amount of restoration was carried out and since 1961 the castle has been maintained as a national monument.

Description

The finest view of the castle's turreted façade is seen from the water. The castle is entirely hidden from visitors who make their way through the village that grew up outside its bounds, providing taverns and married quarters for the garrison. The river dominates the scene. Opposite the castle are the dockyards of Chatham, the successors of the Tudor creation. Downstream, past the magazines, are the bare three masts of the training ship *Arethusa.* Each in its way helps to stimulate the imaginative re-creation of an earlier scene when the ships of the first Elizabeth's Navy Royal lay up with shroudless, sailless masts, 'in ordinary,' under the protective guns of 'the new blockhouse upon the Gillingham Water.'

Even after turning aside from the High Street, the castle is not reached until the eighteenth-century guardroom beside the gate and the now decayed three-storeyed brick barracks are passed. Built soon after 1718, the barracks replaced accommodation formerly provided within the castle but by then taken over to house gunpowder and munitions. They are among the first distinct barracks to be built in England. Few were built in the eighteenth century. Parliament after the experiences under the Stuarts was at first wary lest the monarchy established a standing army and maintained absolute rule. It was careful to see that the army had no fixed accommodation outside the recognised fortresses. Not until after the Industrial Revolution in France did the ruling classes become more afraid of the people, and barracks become useful as police stations. The barracks block at Upnor has changed little externally in 250 years. It figures frequently in drawings and prints and we even have a copy of the architect's original design.

The present castle has emerged from two distinct building periods though this is not immediately obvious. The main building with the water bastion and the river frontage belongs to Sir Richard Lee's design of 1559–67. The two riverside towers were substantially rebuilt and the gatehouse and the moat enclosing the courtyard were added by Arthur Gregory and Baptist nearly fifty years later. The heightening of the river front, giving it a mock-castle effect, and the alterations to the gatehouse and the towers came later in the seventeenth century. The detailed interpretation of these later alterations and, indeed, the original arrangements, will not be possible until archaeological excavation and a close examination of the structure have been made.

Gatehouse (1599–1601)

The dry ditch enclosing the castle was dug in 1599. Originally it was 32ft (9.8m) wide and 18ft (5.5m) deep but it has become partially filled over the years. It could be covered by cannon firing through the arched GUNPORTS low down in the two towers that project from the high stone curtain wall which limits the

Gatehouse from the courtyard

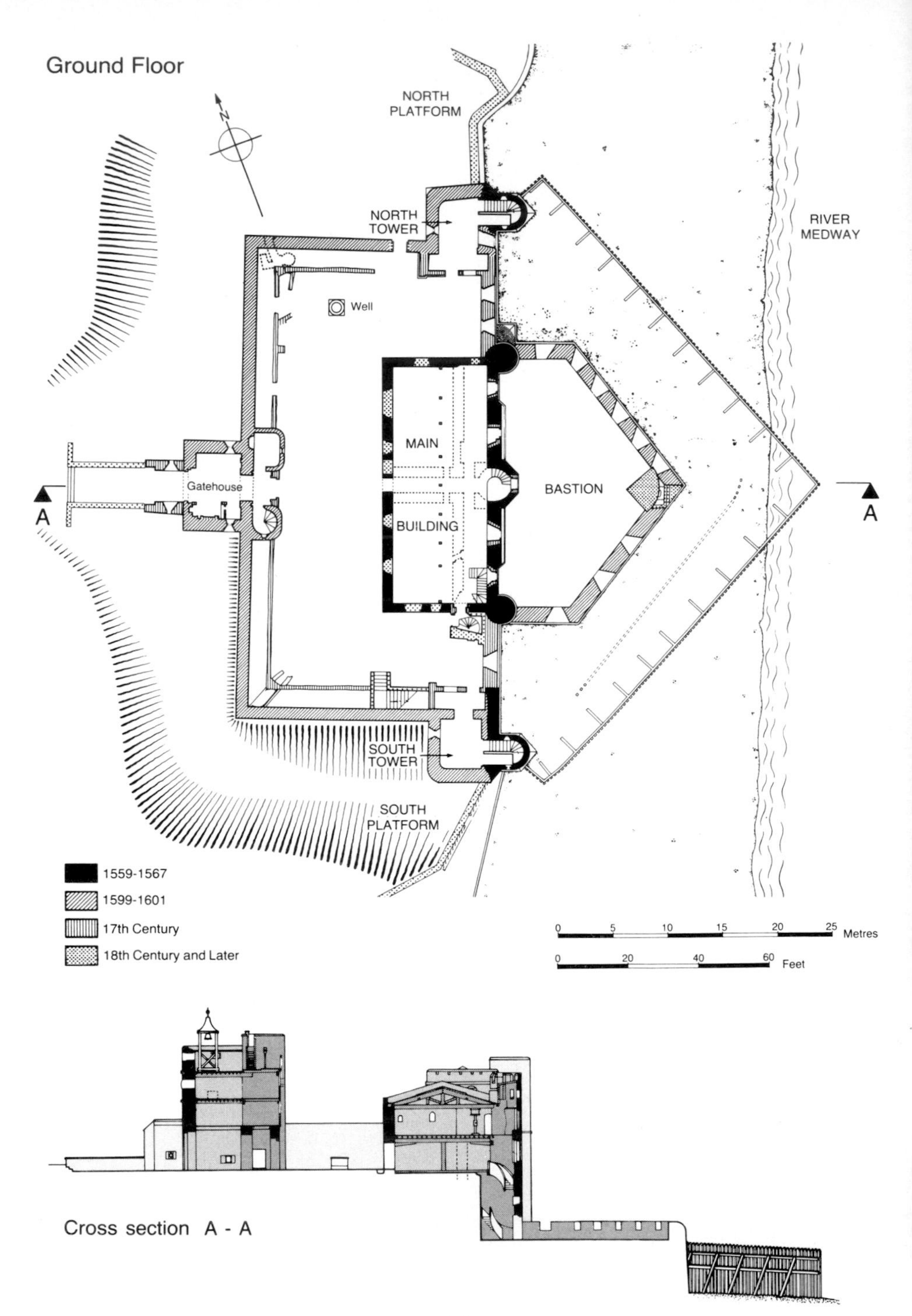
Ground Floor
NORTH PLATFORM
NORTH TOWER
RIVER MEDWAY
Well
MAIN
BUILDING
BASTION
Gatehouse
A
A
SOUTH TOWER
SOUTH PLATFORM
1559-1567
1599-1601
17th Century
18th Century and Later
0 5 10 15 20 25 Metres
0 20 40 60 Feet
Cross section A - A

Basement

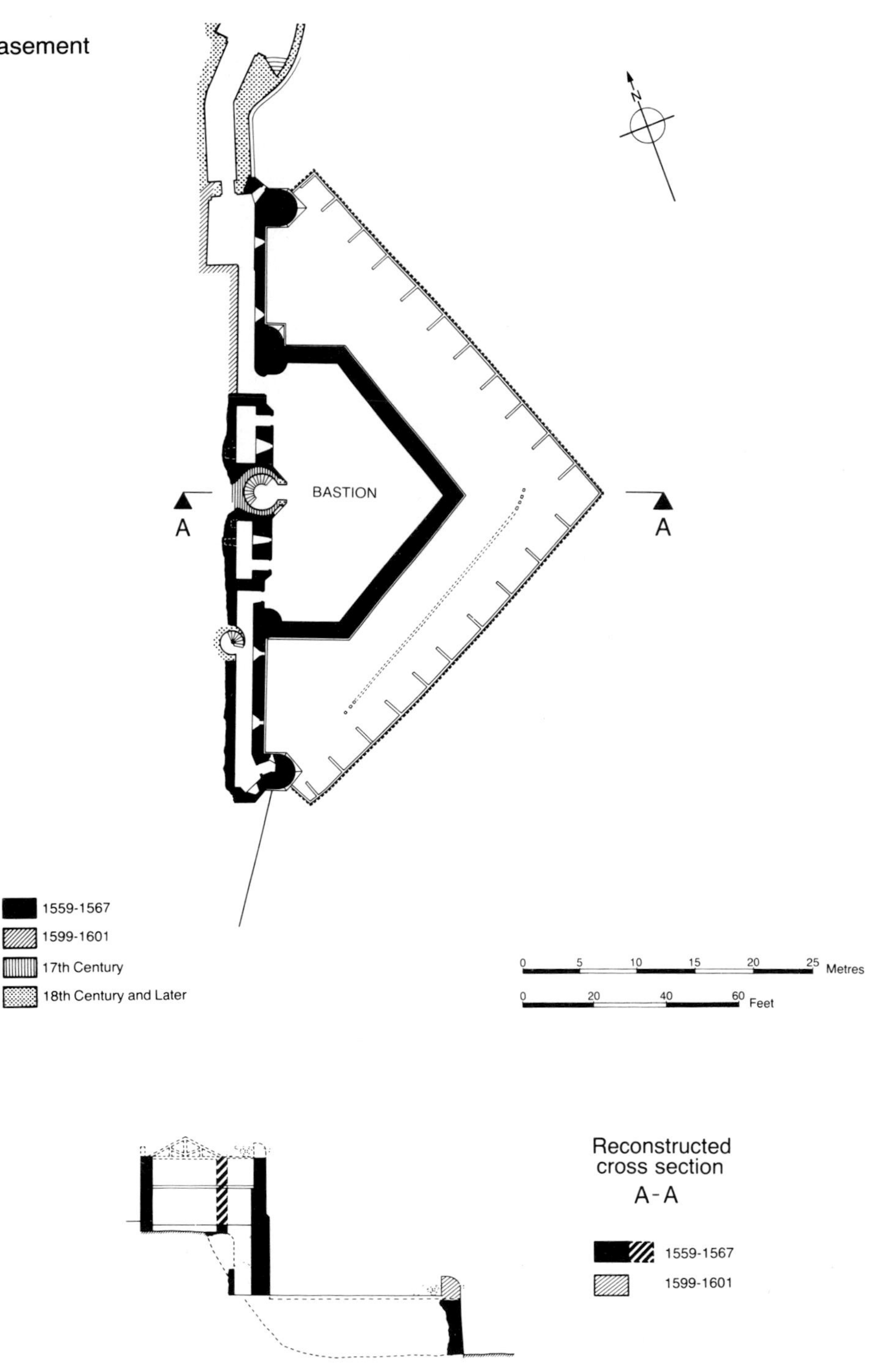

N
BASTION
A
A
1559-1567
1599-1601
17th Century
18th Century and Later
0
5
10
15
20
25
Metres
0
20
40
60
Feet
Reconstructed
cross section
A - A
1559-1567
1599-1601

Line engraving from MS of Thomas Pennant's 'Outlines of the Globe,' volume XX, 1787

courtyard. Two more gunports are in the ground floor of the gatehouse. There is now no sign of the drawbridge that formerly existed here. The flank walls on either side of the entrance were added later and contain very archaic cross-loops as well as being roughly built. Over a lintel, on the right is an inscription 'W Webster XXIII Regt, 1787 May.'

The gatehouse was very much altered in the 1650s, before and after the fire that damaged it so severely. The brickwork is all of that date except where it has been repaired more recently. One reason for the rebuilding must have been to gain extra height. The double-splayed gunports in the parapet, somewhat similar to those in the flanker, were intended to cover the landward approaches. In contrast the clock below them belongs to more secure times. The bell in the wooden bell-cote has the date 1809 on it, and probably the clock is not much older. Immediately above the gate arch is a brick-filled opening or recess, perhaps for a coat of arms or inscription.

Inside the round-headed gateway is a wide entrance passage. The door itself, though old, is not original. The gunports in the flankers are just over 18in (45cm) square, with EMBRASURES splayed inside and out to allow for the traverse of the gun. The sills are socketed to take a pivot. The openness of the entrance has been reduced by the insertion of a large fireplace immediately on the right. It was there in 1725, as was a tiny cubby-hole of a room opposite, the creation of which probably led to the mutilating of the right JAMB of the entrance arch. This partitioning has long disappeared. The main guardroom must have been the small room on the left, lit by two small windows, its fireplace now blocked. The porter could watch the NEWEL stairs opposite, which led to two floors above the entrance passage. The stairs continue up to the gun platform above the roof.

The scorched red stones on the first-floor walls are testimony of the fire of 1653. None of the woodwork in the upper storeys is original and the floor levels have been altered; close to the second-floor level are the blocked remains of three small splayed gunports. In the northeast corner on the second floor is a painting of a ship on the wall plaster. It is thought to have been drawn about 1700, the sprit-sail topmast not having been used in large ships after 1720; there are traces of drawings elsewhere.

The back of the gatehouse was not in this form originally. The rear gateway was at some time pushed outwards to the line of the square turrets projecting from the main tower and open BALUSTRADES placed over it. The latter are modern, but from evidence of old prints something similar existed in the eighteenth century.

Courtyard

Much of the wall enclosing the courtyard was rebuilt after 1625. Inside are the brick foundations of narrow lean-to buildings which added to the storage capacity of the magazine establishment. A late doorway gave access from the gatehouse to the upper floor of the northern range. A drain leads out diagonally through the southwest angle of the curtain wall and in the northwest corner there is a SALLYPORT with an oven beside it. Within the courtyard is the castle well and at each end are large Turkey Oaks, natives of Asia and southern Europe, not introduced into this country until 1735. They are said to have been grown from acorns brought back from the Crimea after the Crimean War. On either side of the entrance into the Main Building are two water tanks dated 1856 and bearing the Board of Ordnance marks and coat of arms.

North and South Towers (1599–1601)

The two waterfront towers are, as one would expect, very similar to the gatehouse. There are the same neat, small, squared, coursed rubble, the same trick of rounding off the corners, and similar gunports for the cannon giving flanking fire down the moat. When built they were two-storeyed and constructed over the remains of Lee's towers. The embrasures on the gun platform on the roof were either blocked or converted into windows when the towers were adapted to make a third floor for accommodation later in the seventeenth century. At the same time they were extended and their backs closed with brickwork. They have also been given low-pitched roofs hidden by a brick parapet.

On the river side the half-round turrets provide room for stairs and, on the ground floor, latrines. These turrets are probably the survivals of Lee's design, at

North Tower from the Water Bastion

least externally, up to the STRING COURSE at first-floor level. They contain early forms of pistol loops, mostly in the form of an inverted keyhole, and one in the South Tower, consisting of two round holes linked by a slit after the fashion of a dumbbell. In both turrets the stairs and latrine passage retain their mid-sixteenth-century door frames, though perhaps these have been reset. The remainder of the towers belong to Gregory's remodelling in 1600–01.

According to Hasted, the South Tower was intended for the use of the governor. The first floor for no clear reason is known as the Queen's Room. The conversion of the South Tower to a residence looks as if it was done later than that of the North Tower. The external steps were added later still. Neither tower lends itself to providing comfortable quarters and is it not surprising that successive governors rejected them. On the outside of the arch leading into the ground floor of the South Tower, the letters T M and the date 1596 are scratched into the stone. This was covered by plaster until the tower was badly shaken by bomb blast. There are detailed accounts for the construction of the flanking towers in 1600–01. This arch may therefore have belonged to the earlier building and been rebuilt into the later tower. There is another inscription on the jamb: IC1677.

Connecting the towers with the main building are two short lengths of wall. The parapets of these curtain walls were raised in 1600–01 and again in the eighteenth century. The parapets of 1600 had a rounded profile like that of the Water Bastion. There are now two embrasures in the north curtain and one in the south, serving three 64-pounder (29kg), rifled muzzle-loading guns of 1859 and 1860. There were additional gun batteries outside the two towers at the end of the ditch as early as 1698. Much of the south platform still remains but its two embrasures have been blocked.

Main building or Magazine (1559–67)

In the centre of the main front is Sir Richard Lee's castle, with its bastion projecting out into the Medway and the large building behind it which later became known as the Magazine. This building has been so altered internally as well as externally that it is now extremely difficult to decide how it functioned or what its appearance was like when it was built.

This, the first castle, must be visualised in profile, for the form of its construction is determined by the fact that it is built out over the river bank. The long oblong range of two storeys, which is entered from the courtyard, oversails the bank so that its outer wall drops down to the shore-line at present below low-water mark. Behind this wall is another, probably REVETTING the early line of the river bank. As a result there is a space for storage or powder magazines between the two walls at the same level as the bastion and continuing as a passage on either side. The line of this rear wall was continued, though stepped back 6½ft (2m) above the ground floor, until it was swept away late in the eighteenth century.

View from the southwest

Whether it went higher, above the first floor, is less certain. It would have been possible for this to have happened, providing space for gun platforms on either side of the centrally placed stair turret at first-floor level, and allowing a second storey for the otherwise limited barrack accommodation behind the guns. At all events a good deal of rebuilding of the upper part of the walls was done afterwards. A distinct break in the masonry style can be seen on the river façade at a level just above the lower line of ROUNDELS. From the small squared, well coarsed and GALLETED rubble of the original work, the masonry changes to larger less-regular rubble without galleting. The change in construction can be followed round at roughly the same level for the rest of the main building.

Great changes were doubtless necessary when it was decided to convert the castle into a magazine in 1668. The original openings where they survive on the river front have typical Tudor four-centred heads. The windows facing the courtyard and those in the upper parts of the river façade are rectangular and

MULLIONED. Remains of windows or gunports of this form can be seen in the masonry high up on the river front where they were blocked later still to allow for the insertion of the roundels. It therefore seems as if, following the conversion, the gun platform over the main building was no longer necessary and in order to gain more storage space for the powder barrels the top storey was extended the full width of the building. Before 1698 the castle thus acquired its present façade, with the decorative roundels, the large round-headed windows in the stair turret, and the elaborate skyline of ornamental battlements to continue the Elizabethan tradition.

Internally, the needs of the magazine have taken precedence. In 1725 the ground floor was still divided into three compartments, two oblong rooms separated by a passage leading from the main door and a narrow passage-like space stretching the length of the building and lit by two splayed loops. The internal partitioning has now gone though there are signs of the end of it on the north wall. Instead, the woodblock floor and copper-sheeted doors (cutting down the risk of sparks) have taken their place.

Drawing of Upnor from William Hogarth's sketchbook

The castle seen from the Medway

Above the round-headed entrance, until recently blocked in favour of a later forced opening, is a space for a coat of arms or plaque but there is nothing of the original detail. The ground floor houses a small Turkish field gun and a German Krupps field gun here mounted on their carriages. There is a case of objects associated with the castle as well as a collection of Romano-British pottery found at various sites along the river. On the floor above, beside the central stair turret, is a windlass for raising stores up to this level. In the opposite wall are the remains, now blocked, of an original fireplace and there are two small blocked openings in the north wall. An exhibition of prints and drawings relates to the development of the Medway defences, the Dutch Raid and Upnor Castle itself.

Water Bastion (1559–67)

The stair turret takes visitors from the ground floor to the platform of the Water Bastion. Here are mounted five 12-pounder (5.4kg), 4½in (114mm) howitzers and a 32-pounder (14.5kg) muzzle-loader belonging to the mid nineteenth century. There are nine embrasures, six facing downstream and three upstream. Against the rounded turrets of the main building can be seen the straight joint of the parapet provided in 1600. Six feet (2m) below, the masonry is bonded into the main structure. The rounded parapet, so built to deflect shot, was a common feature in Henry VIII's castles but seldom used since.

In the face of the main building are three doorways, the two on either side of the stair turret leading into the small chambers which may originally have been served from the stairs. On the south is a similar doorway which leads to the vaulted passage below the curtain extending to the basement of the South Tower. Perhaps the remains of another doorway, now built into the base of the stair turret, belonged at the north where a much larger nineteenth-century doorway gives access to the remodelled vaulted passage to the North Tower. The windows are small with pointed arches. Also on the wall of the main building can be seen the CORBELS and roof-line of the covered structures which occupied the bastion during much of the eighteenth and nineteenth centuries when the gunpowder was brought into the magazine by way of a jetty and through a breach in the SALIENT of the bastion.

Finally visitors should note the successor of the 'palissado' considered so essential in 1599. At low-water the stumps of the previous timbers can be seen indicating that this feature of the castle at least has been continued over three hundred years.

Aerial view from the southeast

Acknowledgements

We acknowledge permission from the British Museum to reproduce the plates on pages 5, 12, 16, 17 and 20 (upper); and from the National Maritime Museum for the plates on pages 8, 20 (lower), 26 and 31.

Glossary

ASHLAR	Squared block(s) of stone
BALUSTRADE	Series of short pillars supporting a handrail
BASTION	Projection from the general outline of a fortress from which the garrison can see, and defend by flanking fire, the ground before the ramparts.
BATTERY	Platform or fortified work on or within which artillery is mounted
BLOCKHOUSE	Small detached fort
BOOM DEFENCE	Barrier consisting of connecting spars, pieces of timber, chain, etc, stretched across a river or harbour mouth to obstruct navigation
BULWARK	Bastion or (in first half of sixteenth century) a blockhouse
CASEMATE	Vaulted chamber built in the thickness of the rampart of a fortress with embrasures for the defence of the place, used as a barrack or battery or both
CHAMFER	Plane produced by bevelling off a square edge
COOPERAGE	Cooper's workshop. A cooper is a craftsman who makes or repairs wooden casks or barrels
CORBEL	Projection from the face of a wall to support a weight

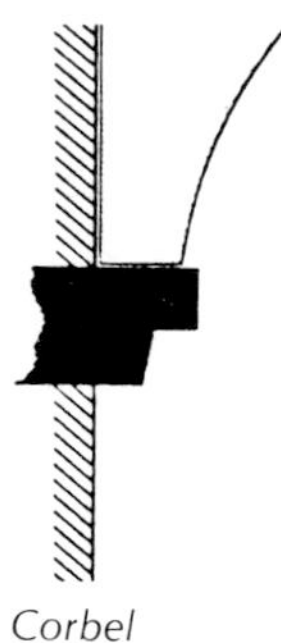

Corbel

CORNPOWDER	Gunpowder that has been granulated
CURTAIN WALL	Wall enclosing a courtyard
DRAWBRIDGE	Wooden bridge which can be raised towards a gateway by means of chains or ropes attached to its outer end
EMBRASURE	Opening in a parapet through which a gun can be fired

FLANKER	Fortified position within a bastion able to provide flanking fire along the line of curtain wall
GALLETING	Insertion of small flints or stones in the mortar joints of masonry
GUNPORT	Opening in a wall for a gun to fire through
HOY	Small sailing vessel usually rigged as a sloop, used for short-distance coastal traffic
LOOP	Narrow vertical slot in a wall for shooting through or admitting light
MATCHLOCK MUSKET	Hand gun whose action depends on the ignition of the powder by means of a burning match
MULLION	Vertical division of a window
NEWEL	Central pillar round which the steps of a winding stair radiate
ORDNANCE	Artillery engines for discharging missiles
Demi-cannon	Heavy-shotted medium-range gun with 6½in bore and throwing 32lb shot
Culverin	Light-shotted long-range gun with 5¼in bore and throwing 18lb shot
Demi-culverin	4½in bore; 8lb shot
Saker	3¾in bore; 6lb shot
Minion	3¼in bore; 4lb shot
Falcon	2¾in bore; 2lb shot
Fowler	Small-shotted short-range piece
PALISADE	Palings of strong timber serving the same function as modern barbed-wire
PLATFORM	Floor on which cannon are mounted
PROOFYARD	Place for testing firearms and explosive
REVETMENT	Retaining wall built to support or hold back a mass of land or water
ROUNDEL	Decorative panel or window in circular form
SALIENT	Angle (usually of a bastion) projecting towards the country
SALLY PORT	Subsidiary opening for troops engaged in a sally (sudden rush of troops from a fortress to attack besiegers)
SCONCE	Small fort or earthwork often built as a strong point to defend some physical feature such as a ford or an entrance
SNAPHAUNCE MUSKET	Hand gun using an early form of flintlock
STRING COURSE	Moulding or projecting band running across the façade of a building or around its walls